THE IN THE SMOKER MINDSET

ERIC L. JOHNSON II

ACKNOWLEDGEMENTS

I have never imagined myself writing a book of any sort. Throughout the past few years, I have been making an extreme push to improve myself mentally, physically, and emotionally. This would not have been possible without the support that my mom, Shirley Bolden, and step dad, Wil Bolden, have provided me. I remember back when I was in elementary school, before my mom would drop us off at school each morning, she would tell me and my brother that we were destined for success. This statement has always encouraged me to do more than the status quo because I always felt that I was meant to do more. Fast forward to now I have taken an unconventional path of creating my own company. I am sure there were concerns, but my mom and Wil have continuously provided unconditional support for me during this journey and this is what keeps me going. So thank you both for continuing to believe in me.

If I am being totally honest, I had severe confidence issues during the whole process of writing this book. I felt like I would not be able to place my thoughts on paper to reflect the message that I was trying to convey. I also felt that people would focus on any mistake that I made in formatting or punctuation used in the book instead of the overall message that I was trying to deliver. NancieLee Fennema willingly helped me make edits to my book that allowed me to feel much more confident in the message that I was conveying. She also ensured me that I was not a bad writer at all and I was just being too hard on myself. That boost in my confidence was a game changer. Her meticulous editing process turned out to be instrumental to the end result of this book. She helped me transform this book into something that I could truly be proud of. I cannot express how thankful I am to her for helping me with this project.

In this book, I talk about surrounding yourself with people that will make you better. Andre Truss is one of those people in my life. I almost quit writing this book about two weeks into the project. I was not confident in the direction that I wanted to take the book, and I was not sure that anyone would care. Not only did Truss give me the figurative slap to the face that I needed, but he also helped me complete the first two rounds of edits on the book to ensure that I was going in the right direction. Thanks for continually pushing me to be better and believing in me when I do not necessarily believe in myself.

Have you ever had a friend that seemed more excited about something you were doing than you were? Paige Hurston was that friend for me. She helped me celebrate any milestone that I hit with this book. She helped me formulate ideas and gave me outside perspectives so that I could continue to convey the correct message to my readers. Everyone needs a friend like her in their corner to keep them encouraged. Thank you for being constant encouragement for me.

This book would not exist without Tellers Pollard. It all started with a conversation in our office back in August. He mentioned that I should create an ebook in order to convey my message to a larger audience beyond social media. I laughed and told him that I was not an author. His response was, essentially, that we can do anything we want and that there was no reason not to write one. Until this conversation, I had never even considered writing a book. After writing this book, I am already planning to write more. I appreciate the idea and the push to just get started.

NOTE FROM AUTHOR

Thank you so much for purchasing my book. If you are anything like me, then you understand the constant struggle of overcoming the fear that no one is listening to you. This internal battle has been extremely intense during the creation of this book, but I believe I have come out on top. I feel substantial growth, not only in my ability to express ideas in a more articulate manner but also in the network of positive people who surround me. This was truly a team effort and I am truly thankful for my team.

It is exciting to think that something I created to give other people confidence in themselves, also gave me confidence in myself as well. I started my company "In The Smoker" because I knew too many people that had dreams and goals that they told themselves they would never be able to achieve. More often than not, this was because they felt like they would not be able to escape the grasp of financial struggles that seemed to plague their lives. How many times have you heard someone express a goal that they were passionate about and immediately dismiss the goal from reality because they did not believe they had the necessary funds available to make it happen?

As I started to really listen to the concerns of people that felt like they were not where they wanted to be in life, I realized that personal finance issues were also causing a multitude of other problems in people's lives. Relationship issues (romantic & non-romantic), physical health issues, mental health issues, were all ways in which financial issues were manifesting themselves in people's lives.

I feel, with a topic as sensitive as personal finance, it is important for the person relaying the information to have the ability to connect and relate to the people they are attempting to help. It is hard to help people find solutions to problems that you have no personal connection with. It is even more difficult when you do not understand issues within the communities that are further compounding certain issues in a person's personal life.

Personal finance can be intimidating for many people, but the only way to overcome any fear is to face it head on. After all, fear can be a real mind bender. I do not think this book will fix everyone's financial problems but what I do want is for this book to encourage people to start having conversations about the topics that have been covered within its pages. We can resolve many of the issues in our lives by not being afraid and just learning to talk about them. I want people to understand that they do not need to have all the answers as long as they know how to find the people that do have the answers.

I want everyone to start doing the following: Identify problems, seek solutions, and take massive action to implement the tools given to you in order to eradicate the problems. We can all be better, and if we learn to work together as an unselfish collective then we will be better much sooner. This is me making an effort to be the change that I want to see. I hope you enjoy the book. Let's get In The Smoker!

TABLE OF CONTENTS

INTRODUCTION

As I sat in my office with one of my Marines, I can remember feeling utterly ashamed. While reviewing the terms and conditions of a payday loan my Marine failed to repay--I quickly realized that I was in no position to help him. This was not because I did not care to help him but rather, because I--and so many others--was no more equipped than he at understanding the intricacies of personal finance. The terminology utilized within the loan paperwork appeared to be a foreign language as I browsed through all the legalese in the voluminous document. As someone who was sworn to protect my Marines, it was during this moment holding those documents, I felt like a failure. In that same moment, I knew I needed to make a change. Not just for my Marines but because I swiftly came to the realization that if I did not make a change, I could easily find myself in the same unfortunate situation.

With that, I decided to research all aspects of personal finance–traditional / contemporary, conventional/cutting-edge, off the beaten path, etc.-- in order to be a resource to those under my charge, improve my own personal finances, and help my family and friends. Since then, I have become a Dave Ramsey Certified Financial Coach, I have also long enjoyed the benefits of financial freedom, and my tribe of financially independent people continues to grow stronger everyday. Unfortunately, at the start of my road to become financially independent, I was ill prepared to find out just how behind the power curve I was and had been. Why did I, a graduate of the United States Naval Academy, have such little understanding about--and thus a lack of control over--the real nature of my financial situation? Part of the reason was that there were no resources in place that emphasized the importance of personal finance during my childhood. Then as an adult blinded by pride, my unwillingness to seek help and just being comfortable with the status quo, also contributed to the financial situation that I knew I needed to overcome. Once I identified the factors holding me back from financial independence, I developed the In The Smoker Mindset, which will help anyone overcome the similarly taunting financial issues that I had faced by focusing on four problematic areas. Later in this book you will read about my friend Gabby, who diligently employed my methods and went from owing more than $80K to having a solid debt payoff plan, with over $11K in her savings account in less than a year.

PERSONAL FINANCE IN THE U.S.

As I began my research, the statistics were overwhelmingly shocking. Did you know that over 50% of Americans live paycheck to paycheck? Imagine wrapping up a full work day expecting to get in your car, decompress, and drive home. As you turn the vehicle on, blinking sensors on the dashboard are a constant reminder that you cannot afford to get your car serviced. As you walk into the house, anxiety fills your body as bill collectors repeatedly call you about a credit card account you have not been able to make even the minimum payment due for the past few months. As you review your bank accounts, you realize your savings account is nothing more than a holding place for the zero that seemingly remains indefinitely. Let us take a breath here and understand that you are not alone--this is reality for half of all adult Americans.

Unfortunately, even more disturbing statistics exist. A prime example contends that fewer than 40% of people have enough in their savings accounts to pay for an unexpected $1,000 emergency expense in cash. This would suggest over 60% of Americans have to take on more debt through the use of a credit card or a small loan in order to cover such an expense. Talk about a rat race. Why are there so many honest, hard-working Americans finding themselves entangled in that rat race? Many people will tell you it is because people are not getting paid enough. I would argue that while important, income and wages are only one piece of the problem. Some of my clients (even after taxes) easily bring home a six-figure salary, but even these well-paid or high-income earners fall into the aforementioned statistical categories. So, if earned income is not the only issue, then what else could the problem be? Over time and through the course of my extensive research, I have determined the overlying problem to be a combination of these four factors: 1) a lack of financial education, 2) an unwillingness to seek help, 3) comfortable with the status quo, and 4) being blinded by pride. Let us review these in greater depth.

Lack of financial education

The first factor is a lack of financial education. Many of my clients were not taught or offered lessons about personal finances growing up. Discussions about finances in the household, especially with children, are critical to setting a solid foundation for a person's financial future. As adults, a lack of education can no longer be an excuse for poor financial decisions. As adults, we are all capable of researching and seeking out the help we need in order to overcome our financial struggles. That being said, adults of all living generations find themselves in the pit of financial despair (see Figure 1 for details about debt by age group). So, while it remains true that some of us may have had a late start gaining financial knowledge, it is now on us, as adults, to shape our financial future. It is never too late to take the path towards financial freedom.

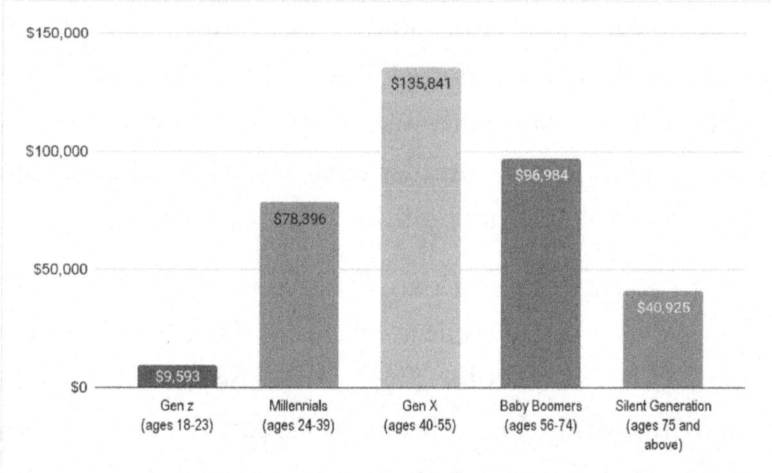

Figure 1. Average Debt Balances by Age Group

Unwilling to seek help

I touched on this factor a little in my previous paragraph, which is, we have to be willing to seek out the help. In all of our lives, there are friends, family, acquaintances, and experts out there with the knowledge, skills, experience, and expertise that you may need in order to overcome not just your financial burdens but many of life's other conundrums. For some reason, our modern society has made seeking help appear to be a negative thing. This thought process has proved to be debilitating and this is particularly evident among African American and other minority communities across the United States. Many of you would be surprised with just how many people would be willing to help if you just asked--contrary to certain beliefs it is not a negative thing to ask for help.

Your debt does not care who gets the glory or the credit. Someone who climbed out of debt on their own is no more spectacular than someone who received help from a friend or a financial coach. The important part is to make the change and get out of debt by using the resources available to help us reach our financial goals. Debt, loan terms and conditions, interest rates, and collections can be tricky and intimidating. Trying to minimize it on your own could turn a six-month plan into a five year journey.

Comfortable with the status quo

I am not sure when people became so comfortable with the status quo, but it is now a visible problem in society. I cannot tell you how many times I have heard someone say, "I can make all of my payments on time, so I am going to prioritize fun over paying off my debts". The YOLO or "you only live once" mentality is a plague when it comes to personal finance. While it may be true that "you only live once", someone juggling debt will experience life very differently than someone who is financially free with no incumberences. Subsequently, I try to get people to see the bigger picture. My sound advice to someone with the "you only live once" mindset, and/or those, for example, who want to prioritize excessive expenditures like travel, or new cars, over paying debts off just because they can pay *all* of their bills on time by paying only the *minimum* amount due is this--if you are willing to make some changes and pay off these debts quickly, then the thousands of dollars that you will save on interest can be used to have more "once in a lifetime" moments in idyllic far away places or more means to buy top notch goods without having to borrow money from anyone.

In short, a shift in priorities is needed. However, identifying the problem is not enough. You need to identify people that can help hold you accountable and not deter you from reaching your financial goals. The behaviors of the people you spend the most time with should ideally emulate the behaviors that you need to practice in order to reach your goals of financial freedom. You will need to step out of the status quo comfort zone and take action in order to make impactful and long-lasting changes.

Blinded with pride

What price are you willing to pay for your pride? I frequently find myself asking people dealing with financial struggles this very question. Some of you may be thinking, what does pride have to do with this? Well in my own personal experiences, anything that I have failed at has been a direct result of my inability to seek the help needed to find a solution. I used to be the classic "I do not need anyone to help me because I can do everything myself" type of person. Painfully, and not without cost, I learned that I could have avoided the disappointment and stress of not knowing what direction to go in by having asked someone knowledgeable about topic x,y, or z for help.

Studies show that the average millennial (ages 24-39) has amassed more than $78,000 worth of debt. So, for the average millennial with the "I can do it myself mentality"--likely struggling and making little to no progress paying off their debts--is it safe to say pride is worth the average $78,000 of debt? Is it also safe to say that these are staggering numbers and this is not just a problem for millennials? As you can see in Figure 1, the average adult from Generation X (ages 40-55) has amassed an even higher debt average of $135,000. The costs of the pride-to-debt ratio is afflicting adults of all generations. No one's pride is worth being indebted to faceless banking institutions, apathetic credit card companies, and tenacious collection agencies for the entirety of their life. It is never too late to swallow your pride, ask for help, and catch your breath. You will be a better person that will find themselves in a better position in life for doing so.

THE IN THE SMOKER MINDSET

The four factors listed above are directly related to the mindset of an individual. As a well-researched and experienced financial coach, I have become very aware of how important a person's mindset is to proper and prosperous financial management. I wanted to find a way to convey the message that before you can master your personal finances you have to master your mindset. This will ultimately help you achieve not only your financial freedom but other life goals as well. I wanted to be able to share this message with everyone that I had the opportunity to help. However, before I could do this, I had to determine what I thought was truly important. During this time of introspection I identified four areas that, if focused on, could help individuals not only with their financial journey but with life in general. The four areas to focus on are concerned with a person's pride, accountability, honesty, and learning to identify and not make excuses. The following paragraphs will explain these four problematic areas in greater detail.

Focus on Pride

The first area to focus on is "pride". Pride is typically a topic that many people would like to avoid. Be that as it may, when it comes to finances, pride is one of the biggest opposers of escaping our financial worries. Stuck behind the helm of pride, I have seen many people allow themselves to stay in a perpetual state of unhappiness. By allowing their pride to be more important than seeking help to get out of whatever situation they were facing, many will find themselves cascading deeper and deeper in debt. If you want to progress and make the most out of this life, then you are going to need help from someone at some point. Not having all the answers is never a bad thing, but pretending you know it all when you do not, just so you feel better about yourself, will not actually help you or your financial situation. The sooner you can put your pride to the side and allow yourself to receive help, the sooner you will begin to see yourself progress towards your goals.

Focus on Not Making Excuses

The second area to focus on can be tricky for some, as we have all been on one end or the other of it in our lives, and that is "making excuses". It is way too easy for us to allow ourselves to make excuses--sometimes without even knowing we are making excuses--and blame anything but ourselves for the reason things are not the way we want them to be. Let me give you an example of how easy making excuses can be when it comes to finances. It is very easy to say you over spent for the month because your friends wanted to go out to eat 10 times and your excuse for doing the same was because you did not want to hurt anyone's feelings, so you just could not say no in those situations. What about justifying an irresponsible purchase with your feelings? Have you ever heard someone mention that they purchased a new vehicle because it would make them feel better? Driving a new car would likely make anyone's day better, but voluntarily placing yourself deeper into debt because you needed a pick me up is not necessarily a responsible practice to upkeep.

If you want to see progress towards meeting your financial goals, you have to be able to consciously quit making excuses by even identifying the hidden or sneaky ones. If you want to achieve your goal of financial independence, you have to gain the ability to hold yourself accountable--even in those emotionally or socially tricky situations where making an excuse would seem easier in the moment. One of the best things I ever did was to consciously quit making excuses and start holding myself seriously accountable for any shortcomings I had in not just my personal finances, but other facets of my life.

Focus on Holding Yourself Accountable

"Accountability" is an extremely important area to focus on during your pursuit of financial freedom. Personal accountability is critical because it is ultimately your job to hold yourself accountable before you can allow someone else to hold you accountable. Personal accountability will help you take responsibility for your actions, learn from mistakes, and overcome the urge to blame others while hiding from your own culpability within the issues that you may experience.

Not many people will find success in reaching their goal to pay off debt if the people they spend the most time with are continuously engaging in behaviors that produce just the opposite effect. Having an accountability partner in this and many other types of situations can be very helpful and important. You can find an accountability partner who is non-judgemental, and outside of your current inner circle whose behaviors and spending habits may financially be doing you more harm than good. It can be exhausting trying to work towards your goals if you do not have anyone around that can help. An accountability partner helps to hold you accountable by helping to keep you motivated, helping to keep track of your progress, and helping to remind you of your goals.

Are you wondering who should be your accountability partner? Find someone with the same mindset as you, or someone that is in the position that you would like to be in to hold you accountable to the goals that you have set for yourself. Be honest with your accountability partner about your progress, as well as your setbacks. Honesty will help maximize the benefits of having an accountability partner. An accountability partner can also help provide suggestions from an outside perspective, which is critical. Many times, people get caught up in the small details and lose sight of the larger picture at hand. An accountability partner will typically have the larger picture in mind, which is an invaluable asset for you to have at your disposal.

You will also have to hold others accountable to your goals as well. This could end up hurting some feelings. Your friends and family may not want to hear that you cannot take a trip because you are trying to pay down your debt, or that you cannot go out to eat next weekend because it does not fit into your monthly budget. You will find that people will always be quick and happy to help you spend money, but not many will come to your aid when you are trying to correct the damage caused, ultimately, by continuously having tried to please them. Those that truly care about you, while disappointed, will understand and should respect your decisions. Know at the end of each day, as those emotionally or socially not so easy decisions are being made by you, it will be okay because by being diligent and accountable in your decisions you will become ever closer to *your* goal of financial independence.

Focus on Being Completely Honest

Honesty is the last area of focus. More specifically, gaining the ability to be completely honest with yourself. We are always taught to be honest with other people, but I do not believe enough emphasis is placed on being truly honest with yourself. Telling yourself that you did enough, when deep down you know you could have done more, does not set up a healthy environment for true and realistic positive growth. If you cannot be honest with yourself then there is, in effect, no logical way that you can be honest with anyone else--be it a significant other, an accountability partner, or a financial coach. In order to make an effective change in our lives, we have to make all of our truths self evident so we can identify the ones that could hinder our progress. Only then we can hold ourselves accountable to make decisions that will bring us closer to the life-changing impact of financial independence.

The tenets of the In The Smoker Mindset, that I teach to family, friends and clients alike, will help teach you how to focus on removing pride from the equation and the incorrect notions that asking for help is a bad thing. This is just not true, asking for help is a good thing. The tenets of the In The Smoker Mindset can help you identify even those seemingly minor or off-chance excuses we all make, at any age, that can cripple us financially. Adopting an In The Smoker Mindset works best when you can truly be honest with yourself and also hold yourself accountable, along with the aid of an accountability partner to help keep track of your progress and help you reach your goals. If you become adept at this mindset, I am confident that you will begin to see positive changes in your life. After your mindset changes, you may start to notice that the kinds of people you surround yourself with begin to change and evolve as well.

BUILDING AN IN THE SMOKER TRIBE

My research and efforts, knowledge and expertise, have allowed me to develop and witness a grand dream I had from the beginning--in my office years ago with one of my Marines--come to life. The grand dream of gathering together an In The Smoker Mindset tribe, that allows individuals to associate themselves with other non-judgmental people dedicated to making positive changes in their own lives, is growing in numbers and strength everyday. Of course, improving personal finances is a huge part of this, but the In The Smoker Mindset promotes all positive lifestyle changes. Looking back, I am sure many of you can recall moments in your life where you now feel you could have prevented a negative outcome if you had known someone with an answer to your question or just had someone who could have helped with your problem. Maybe, just maybe, you would not have purchased the brand new car you did not need with a 10% interest rate, or rented an apartment with an indoor pool you hardly use for 43% of your total monthly income. You see, often the problem is that many people would rather deal with the fallout from poor financial decisions than deal with the hit to their self esteem from being judged or ridiculed for a perceived lack of knowledge. There is nothing like having access to a group of positive and non-judgemental people, like those of the In The Smoker Mindset tribe, that you can reach out to and seek guidance from, or even just bounce ideas off of, and know that their intentions are pure, as well as experienced and knowledgeable. Can you start to envision why I want to do this? Simply put, we are more powerful as a tribe than we are alone.

One of the biggest decisions that all people will make in their lives is who they allow into their personal inner circle. As we progress and start to improve ourselves, and our lifestyles, it may not take long to realize that many people around you are not on the same wavelength or path as you. For example, it is extremely difficult to lose weight when you spend a great deal of time around people that primarily want to eat fast food. Similarly, it is just as difficult to get out of debt, or save money when the people you keep in close or constant company choose to carelessly and excessively spend their money. Reserving a table at the club with friends every weekend when you will probably spend most of your time at the bar, or buying every pair of release date shoes whether you truly like them or not, or going on "I deserve this" shopping sprees with your friends even though you still have other purchases with tags still on them at home are examples of how people can carelessly and excessively spend their money. In these examples, the practices of the group directly contradict the goals that have been set by the individual. So what is the solution?

A big part of the solution is surrounding yourself with like-minded people who are on the same page, or wish to be on a similar path, as you. This may sound simple, but I am here to tell you it is not that simple, but it is worth every effort. If you are anything like me, then you may have a habit of consciously avoiding decisions that will benefit you if they come at the expense of someone else's feelings. After all, who wants to have an uncomfortable conversation with a friend or family member about how *their* habits are negatively impacting the progress that you are trying to make towards your goal(s)? While this could be difficult for many to do, it may be a necessary conversation for some to have. One thing that I have really learned, throughout this process, is that taking the time and making the conscious effort to put yourself first, in order to progress in life, only hurts the people that feel like they are losing control of you. These types of people do not necessarily care about the fact that you are "trying" to improve, just the fact that if you *do* improve, they will no longer be able to keep you in the same negative space. This is a problem I know many of us have seen or experienced. Do not let other people's selfish motives hold you back from your own progress.

Now I am definitely not saying that all or any of your friends and family have hidden motives to hold you back. Some people, who are close to you, may truly not understand the importance of your goals or your reasons, and that is okay. Conversely, you may be pleasantly surprised to find out that if you approach your friends and family with a goal such as becoming debt free and achieving financial independence, some may eagerly want to join you on your journey. This would be ideal, because that means you would all get to experience growth and financial freedom together. Imagine, for example, group chats with your inner circle are now excitedly centered around who saved the most money for the month or who paid off the most towards their debts, instead of, for example, sending links to overly priced shoes. As a result of this group effort, you will all get to experience the benefits of enjoying financial freedom, you will all be more insync and cohesive as a group, and I would go as far to say that your personal ties and bonds with each other will be stronger and closer than before.

If you cannot find anyone in your current inner circle that wants to participate in your journey, then it may be time to venture outside of that circle. There is nothing more encouraging than being surrounded by people that are all dedicated to improving their lives positively. Finding new people to associate with in this great big world does not have to be difficult. With the age and ease of social media, sometimes it is as easy as posing a question on your Instagram story and seeing what responses you get. At the end of the day, it does not matter how you do so, but you need to make certain that your circle of family and friends is there to help support each other's goals.

THE CHANGE IS FOR YOU, AND ONLY YOU. JUST ASK GABBY.

I have a friend that for confidentiality purposes we will refer to as Gabby. Gabby was able to learn the value of surrounding herself with the right people first hand. Gabby's path towards financial independence began when she lived in a city with an extremely high cost of living, in an expensive apartment that she despised but could not afford to leave due to her financial situation. Living paycheck to paycheck, Gabby--like 60% of all adult Americans--had less than $1,000 in her savings account and--in-step with her Millennial generation--had amassed almost $80,000 in debt. This financial strife, coupled with, or even causing, other unwanted situations in Gabby's life, led to a significant battle with depression and anxiety.

In certain ways, I believe she felt stuck or without options. Gabby did not have anyone nearby to help her overcome this situation because the majority of people she spent time with were in the exact same financial situation. To make matters worse, many of those people just accepted their situation as status quo, while others were just too proud to ask for help. After all, it is hard to point out a problem to someone that does not know the problem exists, and even harder for those who know the problem exists but would rather ignore it than "look bad".

Eventually, and much to my surprise, Gabby reached out to me and asked for help. Gabby was decidedly as ready as ever to make a change and reach her goal of financial independence. I was humbled that she would trust me enough to help with her personal finances and we went right to work. We started by evaluating all of her known personal financial data.

The first thing I wanted to do was to review her weekly, monthly, or yearly budgets. As I had expected, Gabby did not maintain any physical outlines or copies of her budget because, like many others, she attempted to keep all those numbers and goals in her head. Gabby also did not maintain a physical budget because she felt overwhelmed by the number of budget types and templates available and she did not know which one was the best or most accurate. This was a reasonable and common concern, and one I knew we would have to overcome before moving forward. I explained to her that the format of the budget does not necessarily matter as long as you can readily depict the information that you need in order to keep track of your money properly. These initial steps were very critical to building a solid foundation that would ensue financial freedom. I also worked on helping her create a *zero-based budget,* ensuring that she not only understood the process, but felt comfortable enough to execute it on her own. By maintaining a physical copy of the zero-based budget she would be able to account for every dollar, and certify that every available dollar was dedicated towards something that would help achieve her goal of financial freedom whether it be rent or a credit card payment.

By filling out her zero-based budget daily Gabby was able to track her spending in real time, while also holding herself swiftly accountable to the money she had actually spent versus the amount she had budgeted for. During this process, Gabby would also see all of her active debts and her plan to pay them off on a regular and routine basis. Budgeting--with a physical copy--would be key to preventing her from pretending the problem (debt) did not exist by increasing her awareness and thus improving her focus on fixing the problem (debt). These budgeting methods were--for more than a single reason--a real eye-opening experience for Gabby.

First, Gabby realized that she was actually doing a terrible job of keeping track of her actual spending habits in her head. For example, Gabby told me she only spends approximately $120 a month eating out.

After going through her bank statement from the previous month, we were able to conclude that she actually spent over $600 that month eating out. This was a huge disparity. I do not believe many people need to be reminded of the fact that, when it comes to your money, every dollar is important. One of the things that actually caught me off guard was the fact that Gabby had multiple bills--some being paid by autopay setups--that she could not remember what they were for and/or when they were due. This happens to be much more common than you may think. In fact, most of my clients have multiple bills they are paying towards monthly even though they have completely forgotten what or why they were even paying for it originally.

After analyzing Gabby's spending habits and putting those numbers down in black and white on a budget sheet, we started to spot and identify her problem spending areas. The three areas that Gabby overspent the most in were rent, eating out, and shopping. These are typically the high spending areas for the majority of my clients, and these are also typically some of the hardest to get under control. This is not necessarily because these areas are harder to lower your spending towards, but more because people have a difficult time making sacrifices. These are also often activities that are done in a group setting. Are you noticing a theme yet? I wanted Gabby to notice and understand that in order to see the financial progress she desired, she was going to have to start making some sacrifices as soon as possible.

My first recommendation for Gabby was that she find a new place to live with roommates to split the cost of rent. This would allow her to spend less on housing, which she could then allocate the extra money, saved from lowered rent or housing costs, towards her debts and into her savings account. Gabby's current rent was roughly 53% of her take home pay. It is always my recommendation that my clients spend no more than 25% - 35% of their monthly income on housing. The second recommendation was for Gabby to drastically lower the amount she spends on eating out, by deleting all of her food delivery apps and preparing meals from home during the week . The third recommendation for Gabby, specifically, was no more shoe shopping. While some would think I would have received the most pushback from Gabby for the first suggestion, the roommate idea, she was actually more upset about not being able to buy future pairs of Nike's release date Jordans. Given the same set of recommendations, a foodie may have been the most upset about having to give up meals from their favorite restaurants. The sacrifices of a person, whose goal is to be financially independent, are individual and varied, but can also fall into similar categories of poor financial decisions.

After we developed a plan and ways to control Gabby's spending, we had to come up with another plan that would help to pay off her debts. I decided that the *debt snowball method* would be best for her situation. This method prioritizes paying off the smallest debt amounts first, regardless of the interest rate. Some people have argued that this method does not make financial sense because you would still be paying high interest rates on your other accounts. However, on several occasions, I have witnessed that from a mental and emotional standpoint, the debt snowball method is extremely effective for people that are trying to build the confidence to handle their finances expeditiously. I believe this is because by paying off the smaller debts first, people begin to gain confidence in *their* ability to pay off *their* debts, and often start attacking higher debts with more tenacity.

After we finished developing Gabby's financial plan, I checked in with her weekly, as well as on the dates that she had set to meet certain financial goals. We both understood and knew that accountability was going to be critical to the long-term success of her new financial plan. Because it was continuously her biggest monthly cost, since the initial recommendation was made, I repeatedly asked Gabby what her plan was for housing.

All the while, hoping someday soon to hear that she planned to implement the recommendation that I had given her. Unfortunately, in the beginning, this is not what she repeatedly told me.

Gabby, instead, told me something that I know many of us have dealt with at some point. Gabby had family members and close friends who were actually discouraging her from moving, despite the fact that doing so could save her hundreds of dollars every month. Even though she had identified two friends to live with that would undoubtedly support her progress, her family and friends repeatedly told her that changing her current living arrangement and moving in with roommates was a bad idea. From the outside looking in, it appeared some of Gabby's family and friends were not concerned with her goals, but rather, were more concerned with placing their own fears onto her. After a long discussion with me one day, Gabby realized that this decision was for her, and would primarily help her and not really affect them. Some of her family and friends were not happy with her decision, but be that as it may she eventually made the move and was elated with her decision. Gabby's move, and implementation of the initial recommendation, immediately resulted in her rent decreasing from $2,000 a month to $600 a month. As such, she was able to increase her available cash flow by $1,400 every month.

Let us fast forward several months later, to a time when Gabby has started paying off most of her debts and has also been able to put over $11,000 into her savings account. Gabby is more social now and has people around her that she knows she can go to whenever she has an issue and they will go to any means to help her find a solution. The positive outcomes experienced by Gabby in the past several months all started as a financial decision but, again, ended up positively impacting her entire life.

I share this story to remind people that sometimes you just know when you are making the right decision. Other people in your life may not understand your decision, but remember the change is for you, not for anyone else. Just ask Gabby. Do not let people ever convince you that your goal of financial freedom and plans for progression are flawed or wrong. If you feel in your gut that it is the right decision for you, then only you can make it happen. The majority of the people who are telling you not to proceed with your plans, will also not likely be there to help you if you follow their advice and end up in a bad situation. Believe in yourself, do this for yourself, and be resolute. All of us can be like Gabby if we truly want to be and enjoy the same benefits of financial independence.

WHAT IS IN THE SMOKER?

Experiences like the one I had with Gabby, and countless others, are what led to my desire to create a company that would allow me to do what I did for her on a much larger scale. I weighed the option of offering my services as a financial advisor, but I felt like people would be discouraged from working with me because people typically look for a financial advisor when they have a sizable amount of assets and want to make investments. I came to the conclusion that financial coaching was a better option. Being a financial coach would allow me to focus on people who want to get to the point financially where they too could be able to work with a financial advisor. I also wanted to work with "the forgotten" and give them hope.

Dave Ramsey offered a Financial Coach Master Training Course from which I earned the Ramsey Certified Financial Coach Certification. After obtaining this certification, I had to figure out how to create a company that represented values that I felt were important, and create a name for the company that was much more than just a name. So I asked myself what are some of the things I love? Well, I really love to cook. I love everything about cooking including the process, the balance of intuition, art, and science, the tools and labor involved, and I most definitely love enjoying the fruits of that labor. My favorite thing to do on the weekend is being outside over the smoker, smoking various cuts of meat. There is something about smoking meats--the curated, but also intuitive, and slow process to perfection has always been poignant to me and this resonatation led me to the concept behind the "In The Smoker Mindset".

The first thing I do, before I can light my smoker or grill, is go shopping for the meat I am going to cook. When I shop, I am looking for the slab of ribs with the most potential. I am searching for a steak with the best marbling. I am going to put my purchase to good use by using it to fuel and feed myself and the people around me. My clients, and you yourself, possess the same potential. Fully capable of being a better version of themselves, with all the potential to make those around them better as well. However, unrefined, or undercooked, you can actually be dangerous or toxic to those you love.

Once I pick the protein, I take it home and prepare it for smoking with various seasonings. Seasoning gives each cut of meat that I put in the smoker a very specific flavor profile. When I sprinkle the right seasonings onto the meat, I know that when the meat is cooked and ready to consume the flavor will be amazing. I know that not only will this meat feed and fuel myself and others, but the experience of eating this meal will be delicious and exciting too!

Your personal and financial seasonings include, but are not limited to, your habits, your experiences, your drive, etc. These factors, all combined together, make you what you are or give you your specific flavor profile. When you mix the right personal and financial seasonings of habits into your untapped potential, you will create a recipe for positive influence. When your habits are left unchecked or out of balance, you will incur negative effects and possibly become dangerous or toxic to those around you. Adjusting some of your habits and re-aligning your drive will make your life--and the lives of people you care about--more fulfilling.

After the meat has been carefully prepared with the right amount of seasonings, I finally get to put all of my hard work into the smoker. The process is not fast. In fact, it generally takes me a full day just to cook one meal. But that is the beauty of the smoker--it takes patience, consistency, and a watchful eye, but the results are amazing and worth every effort! Unfortunately, the concept of something taking time to manifest has been lost amongst us. With social media, and things like Amazon, instant gratification has become an expectation in all aspects of our lives. However, this is not reality. One of the most important aspects of the "In The Smoker Mindset" is that it takes time to adapt, implement, and effectively improve your circumstances.

The In The Smoker Mindset exists to help you unleash the potential you have within. That potential is going to help you build the life you always wanted and lead you and your family to a life of prosperity for years to come. The In The Smoker Mindset is going to help you turn those pressures in life into the best things that have ever happened to you.

This is more than a brand. The In The Smoker Mindset is a lifestyle.

ARE YOU WILLING TO MAKE THE CHANGE?

Having financial freedom is a blessing that every person should be able to experience. But, in order to be able to enjoy the opportunities that come with financial freedom, people need to take a deeper look at their current relationship with their personal finances and decide to make some major changes and sacrifices. Here is some additional advice to help get you on the right track towards not just financial independence, but a more positive lifestyle overall:

- Stop listening to people who tell you not to seek help just because they did not need or ask for help in their life.
- Stop letting people convince you that utilizing resources that were made available specifically to help you--and many others--is the wrong decision for you.
- Stop letting people make you feel guilty for putting yourself and your future first.
- Stop making excuses for yourself and take ownership of your own shortfalls.

- Stop looking down on others because the route that they are taking to reach their goal may be different than yours.
- Be more supportive of your friends and family when they voice a goal and do your part to help them work towards those goals.
- Be willing to ask for help and seek out information.

As J. Cole hinted in his song "Pride is The Devil" released in 2021, pride can be destructive, and it will continue to be responsible for our setbacks until you find a way to overcome it. We all know we all need a little work, and hopefully this book motivates you to start putting in the work. You have the potential to become the best version of yourself that you never thought was possible. By taking steps to unlock this potential and adopting the "In The Smoker Mindset" not only will you prosper from the changes, but your family, friends, and strangers will benefit as well. You deserve to experience the luxuries living in financial freedom can bring about and all it really takes is making the firm decision to start.

I will leave you with this question. Are you sincerely happy with where you are right now financially? If your answer is anything but a resounding yes, then there is no better time than now to adopt the "In The Smoker

Mindset". We can all be better, and there is nothing better than progressing as a community. Let us develop a plan together to help get you on the fast track to financial freedom and independence and then, the next time someone notices something different about you, just smile and tell them that you are In The Smoker! This is where it starts!

IN THE SMOKER FINANCIAL EVALUATION WORKSHEET

In this section, you will rate your current performance in each area based on a scale of 1-10. Ten being extremely satisfied and 1 being extremely unsatisfied. In each box, write down what is causing you to feel this way along with how to change it or sustain it.

Knowledge of personal finance:

1 2 3 4 5 6 7 8 9 10

Current monthly net take-home pay: ______________

1 2 3 4 5 6 7 8 9 10

Do you maintain a monthly budget? If not, explain why. Is this currently preventing you from reaching your goals?

1 2 3 4 5 6 7 8 9 10

Do you have an emergency fund that can protect you financially for 3-6 months?

What amount do you currently have saved?:

Imagine if you lost your current job and could not find work for six months. Would you have enough money to cover your expenses? Rate your current saving efforts below.

1 2 3 4 5 6 7 8 9 10

Do you have long term savings? If so, is it where you want it to be? This is separate from your emergency fund. ______________________________

1 2 3 4 5 6 7 8 9 10

Are you satisfied with your current spending habits?

1 2 3 4 5 6 7 8 9 10

Willingness to make sacrifices for your financial goals:

1 2 3 4 5 6 7 8 9 10

Your current debt payoff progress:

1 2 3 4 5 6 7 8 9 10

Evaluate your current housing situation. Do you currently rent or own? If you rent, is your current financial situation keeping you from purchasing a home? If you own, are you happy with your current home? If not, are your finances keeping you from getting a home that you truly desire?

1 2 3 4 5 6 7 8 9 10

List the total balances due for all that may apply:

1. Credit cards: ________________
2. Student Loans: ________________
3. Car: ________________
4. Other loans: ________________
5. Other debts: ________________

This section is going to require you to be honest with yourself. The goal here is to help you identify who you need to speak to and what you need to do in order to meet your financial goals.

List 3 people in your immediate circle that you can use to help hold you accountable to your financial goals. This is going to require you to be really and truly honest with yourself. If you cannot name anyone, that is okay. You know that you will need to start looking for new people to add to your circle with the same mindset/goals as you.

1. ________________________________
2. ________________________________
3. ________________________________

List 3 people outside of your current circle that you can use to help hold you accountable to your financial goals.

1. ______________________________
2. ______________________________
3. ______________________________

List at least 3 financial goals for yourself. These need to be goals that you can directly influence. An example of this would be to pay off your Discover Card within the next three months or only spend $150 eating out this month.

1. ______________________________
2. ______________________________
3. ______________________________

What is your current financial situation preventing you from doing? Think in terms of things like taking a vacation, or buying your first home, etc.

Identify 3 areas in which you can lower your spending. How do you plan to implement this plan to spend less in these areas? Which area would be the easiest to start with and why? Which would be the most challenging and why?

1. ______________________________

2. ______________________________

3. ______________________________

How does your current financial status from above look? Are you where you want to be? If not, what is your plan to change this? Write down your plan below.

Made in the USA
Monee, IL
04 November 2026

67384069R00030